SPORTS HALL OF FAME

KEN GRIFFEY, JR.

PEYTON MANNING

SERENA WILLIAMS

VENUS WILLIAMS

GRANT HILL

MICHELLE KWAN

by Lorraine Jean Hopping and
Christopher Ega...

Photos researched by Sylvi...

PHOTO CREDITS—AP/WIDE WORLD PHOTOS: cover (Peyton Manning, Venus and Serena Williams), pp. 3 (all photos), 8 (all photos), 12, 13, 14, 15, 17, 18, 19 (both photos), 20, 21 (top), 23, 25, 29, 30, 31, 33, 35, 38; The Seattle Times: pp. 7, 10; ALL-SPORT USA/Scott Halleran: cover, pp. 4, 5; ALLSPORT USA/Doug Pensinger: pp. 9, 27; ALLSPORT USA/Mark Lyons: p.11; ALLSPORT USA/Stephen Dunn: cover (Grant Hill), pp. 26, 28; ALLSPORT USA/Jed Jacobsohn: cover (Michelle Kwan), pp. 34, 40; ALLSPORT USA/Clive Brunskill: p. 37; ©Franck Seguin, TempSport/CORBIS: p. 21 (bottom); © Wally McNamee/CORBIS: p. 39.

For information contact:
MONDO Publishing
980 Avenue of the Americas,
New York, New York 10018
Visit our web site at http://www.mondopub.com
Printed in Hong Kong
00 01 02 03 04   9 8 7 6 5 4 3 2 1

Interior design by Arlene Schleifer Goldberg
Cover design by David Neuhaus/NeuStudio, Inc.
Photo research by Sylvia P. Bloch
Production by The Kids at Our House

ISBN 1-57255-776-1
Library of Congress Cataloging-in-Publication Data available upon request

CONTENTS

CHAPTER 1
Ken Griffey, Jr.

All-Around Baseball Great

KEN GRIFFEY, JR.

TEAMS: SEATTLE MARINERS, CINCINNATI REDS

HOMETOWN: CINCINNATI, OHIO

BIRTH DATE: NOVEMBER 21, 1969

HE IS A GREAT FIELDER. HE HITS HOME RUNS. AND HE DOES IT ALL WITH A BIG, WIDE GRIN.

Ken Griffey, Jr., grew up around baseball stars. Rickey Henderson stole more bases than anyone. Johnny Bench was a Hall of Fame catcher. Among those great players was Ken Griffey, Sr., Junior's father.

To Junior, sports stars were normal guys. They were friends of his dad. Junior played with their kids. And Major League baseball? To Junior, it was just a fun game.

Rickey Henderson knew better. He told Junior, "You're going to be in the majors someday. Stay away from the wrong crowd."

Rickey was right. At age 19, Junior joined the Seattle Mariners.

Junior was like Superman on a ball field.
His bat swing was fast and smooth, like
his dad's swing. He caught long fly balls
in deep center field. He reached high
above fences to rob hitters of home runs.

For the son of a famous player, baseball was almost *too* easy. Junior often fooled around at practice. As a joke, he wore his cap backward.

Some players thought Junior did not work hard enough. But to Junior, having fun was part of the game. He played better when he smiled. So he made sure he smiled a lot.

In 1990, Ken Griffey, Sr., joined Junior's team for a season. It was the first time a father and son played together in major league baseball.

By 1999, at age 29, Junior had hit 398 home runs. Not even Hank Aaron had 398 home runs at age 29. Hank holds the record for the most home runs in a career at 755.

In 2000, Junior and Senior teamed up again. Junior switched from the Seattle Mariners to the Cincinnati Reds in order to be closer to his family. Ken Griffey, Sr., is now one of Junior's coaches.

With Dad at his side, will Junior beat Hank Aaron's home run record? Maybe. But win or lose, he will have fun playing.

CHAPTER 2

Peyton Manning

Football's Rising Son

PEYTON MANNING

TEAM: INDIANAPOLIS COLTS
HOMETOWN: NEW ORLEANS,
LOUISIANA
BIRTH DATE: MARCH 24, 1976

HIS DAD WAS A GOOD QUARTERBACK.
PEYTON IS THE NEXT GREAT
QUARTERBACK.

In 1998, the Indianapolis Colts picked Peyton Manning first. They wanted him above all other college football players.

Peyton had to choose a number for his first pro jersey. The choice was easy. Peyton picked 18, his father's number. Archie Manning played pro football for 14 years.

Like his dad, Peyton Manning is a quarterback, the team leader. But father and son are not exactly alike. Archie liked to scramble. He twisted and spun his body to avoid tacklers. Peyton likes to stand and pass the football.

Archie played for Ole Miss, the University of Mississippi. Peyton chose the University of Tennessee. He finished college in three years. Most people, including his dad, take four years.

Though done with classes, Peyton could play college football for one more year. Or, he could earn millions of dollars as a pro.

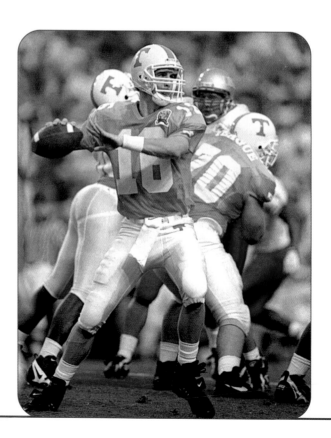

Many pro players told Peyton to take the money. Peyton asked Michael Jordan, a basketball star, what to do.

Michael left college to be a pro. But he told Peyton not to listen to other people. "Do what *you* want to do," Michael said.

Peyton went back to Tennessee. He did not earn a dime playing football that year. But he led his team to a winning season.

In all, Peyton set 33 football records in college. As a pro, Peyton is on his way to setting new records. His goal is to be as good as his dad. Many people say he will be even better.

CHAPTER 3
Venus and Serena Williams
Sisters in Tennis

VENUS WILLIAMS

HOMETOWN: LOS ANGELES, CALIFORNIA
BIRTH DATE: JUNE 17, 1980

AT AGE 14, SHE PLAYED THE TOP WOMEN IN THE WORLD. BY AGE 18, SHE <u>WAS</u> ONE OF THE TOP PLAYERS IN THE WORLD

SERENA WILLIAMS

HOMETOWN: LOS ANGELES, CALIFORNIA
BIRTH DATE: SEPTEMBER 26, 1981

SHE PLAYED HER FIRST TENNIS CONTEST AT AGE 4. AT 17, SHE WON ONE OF THE BIGGEST CONTESTS IN THE WORLD.

Two sisters, Venus and Serena Williams, have a dream. They dream of being the best two tennis players in the world. Which sister will be number one: Venus or Serena?

Both Venus and Serena say that the order does not matter. The Williams sisters, number one and two in the world. *That* is what counts.

Venus is a year older than Serena. But Serena was the first Williams sister to win a major contest. In 1999, she won the U.S. Open. The U.S. Open is one of the four Grand Slam tournaments, the hardest contests to win.

The next year, Venus won Wimbledon, another Grand Slam tournament. To win, she had to defeat the world's top players, including her sister.

Both sisters hit the tennis ball very hard. But Venus hit the fastest serve ever made by a woman! The serve is the first shot of a point.

Venus and Serena grew up in a big city and in a big family. Their father, Richard, first taught tennis to their three older sisters. Then came Venus and Serena's turn.

The two young girls played hard and played well. Venus hit so many tennis balls that her father had to make her rest. She did not want to stop playing!

At age 10, Venus won a big contest for 12-year-old girls. Serena won the same contest the next year.

Venus and Serena became so good that the Williams family moved to Florida. There, the sisters took lessons from a top coach.

They stopped playing contests. Instead, the girls practiced for six hours almost every day.

At age 14, Venus became a pro player. A pro earns money for winning. At first, Venus lost a lot. But as she got bigger and better, she won more matches.

Then Serena turned pro. She wore beads in her hair, just like Venus. Now, the sisters want to defeat everyone. Everyone, that is, but each other!

CHAPTER 4
Grant Hill

Basketball Leader

GRANT HILL

TEAMS: DETROIT PISTONS, ORLANDO MAGIC
HOMETOWN: RESTON, VIRGINIA
BIRTH DATE: OCTOBER 5, 1972

HE STANDS TALL AMONG BASKETBALL PLAYERS.

A basketball team has twelve players. But often, one player stands above the rest. For the Detroit Pistons, that player is Grant Hill. Why do people look up to Grant Hill?

At 6 feet 8 inches, Grant is very tall.
But "look up to" also means to respect or
admire a person. People respect Grant
because he is a great player *and* a great guy.

Grant is not loud or mean on the court.
Instead, he tells players on the other team,
"Nice move." Grant does not dance or show
off after making a basket. But he *does* sign
lots of autographs for fans.

Grant learned good manners from his mother, Janet, and his father, Calvin. Calvin Hill played football with the Dallas Cowboys. His team won the Super Bowl in 1972, the same year Grant was born.

As a boy, Grant did not play football. He chose basketball as his main game.

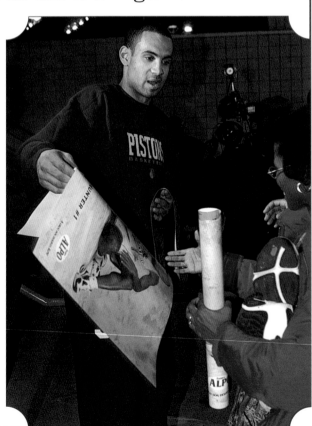

In college, Grant played for Duke University. In a national tournament, the Duke Blue Devils were one point behind Kentucky. They had two seconds to make a basket and win. How short is two seconds? Say, "Duke Blue Devils" twice. That takes about two seconds.

Grant threw the ball from one end of the court to the other. The long pass was perfect. Grant's teammate, Christian Laettner, caught the ball. Just in time, Christian took a shot. He scored!

Duke won the game and, later, the tournament. It was Grant's second national title.

In 1994, Grant joined the Detroit Pistons. He was voted "Rookie of the Year." In 2000, he joined the Orlando Magic.

Grant is often the "go-to guy" near the end of a close game. That means players pass him the ball, and he takes the last shot.

Win or lose, Grant Hill is a team leader.

CHAPTER 5
Michelle Kwan

Skating for Gold

MICHELLE KWAN

TEAM: UNITED STATES OF AMERICA
HOMETOWN: TORRANCE, CALIFORNIA
BIRTH DATE: JULY 7, 1980

SHE WAS THE BEST SKATER IN THE
WORLD AT AGE 15. BUT STAYING ON
TOP WAS EVEN HARDER.

Like a swan, Michelle Kwan glides over the ice. She flies and twirls, her face glowing. Michelle loves to skate—and it shows.

Michelle and her older sister, Karen, grew up skating. Ron, the oldest child, played hockey. At age 7, Michelle won her first gold medal, the top prize in skating. The other skaters were taller and older. Michelle looked like a doll next to them.

By age 12, Michelle did not want to be a cute little doll. She wanted to be a great skater. So she began skating in contests for grown women.

Her heroes were Nancy Kerrigan, Peggy Fleming, and, most of all, Brian Boitano. All three skaters won gold medals in the Olympic games.

In 1996, at age 15, Michelle won the world skating title. But the next year, she fell while doing a triple jump. She came in second behind Tara Lipinski, a younger skater.

The fall made Michelle work harder. She won more gold medals. By 1998, most people thought she would win the Olympic gold, too.

At the Olympics, Michelle skated well. But Tara Lipinski skated better. Again, Michelle came in second. Later that year, at age 17, Michelle won her second world title. But she still did not have an Olympic gold medal.

The next Olympics would be in 2002. That meant four more years of long practices. It meant skating the same moves over and over until they were perfect.

Michelle had an easier choice. She could skip the Olympics. Then she could earn more money skating in shows. But Michelle chose to skate for the Olympic gold. She also chose to earn a college degree. Both goals would take a lot of hard work.